IE Survival Guide Standard II

Categorization
Numerical Progressions
Family Relations
Temporal Relations
Illustrations

Dr. Lynn Brown

This book is dedicated to my family and friends who encouraged me to learn and push my own thinking so that I may have a significant impact on others.

It is also dedicated to my colleagues who believe in the malleability of the human brain and that thinking should be explicitly taught instead of just caught.

Copyright © 2012 by Frameworks, LLC. All rights reserved.
ISBN 978-0-9884091-1-8

Table of Contents

Overview……………………………………………….4

Categorization……………………………. . .. . …..6

  Numerical Progressions……………………………21

Family Relations………………………………………51

Temporal Relations……………………………….....76

Illustrations……………………………………… 100

IE Survival Guide
Standard II
Overview

This booklet is an unauthorized guide and in no way supplants the Instrumental Enrichment Teacher's Guide. Instead it is intended to be a help to the classroom teacher during their first year of implementation. These are my observations and experiences from my first year of teaching IE with helpful input from a teacher colleague. Each instrument begins with an introduction of the overall goal(s) of the instrument, followed by possible ways to teach the cover page, then aids for teaching each page. The aids for specific pages are divided into three parts:

1. Things to Consider – important ideas/concepts on each page.
2. Work on the Sheet – some possible ways to introduce the page and discussions you may want to have as you work with students.
3. Closure - Discussion for Insight – possible topics you may want to cover. Remember this depends entirely on your class discussion and you may not even cover the suggestions stated here but your conversation may lead to something else.

Overall Goal of IE: Make the learner more changeable, open to learning, and self-regulated. They become AWARE and more in charge of their own learning.

Instrumental Enrichment is not just about getting the correct answers. You are teaching **cognitive behaviors** or thinking skills as found in the Process Standards of the Common Core State Standards (CCSS). These cognitive behaviors are aligned to the following sources in the CCSS:

<u>English Language Arts</u>
Qualities of Students Who Are College and Career Ready in Writing, Speaking and Listening
<u>Mathematics</u>
Characteristics of Mathematically Proficient Students

The student must be an active participant in this process of change. It is your job to increase the student's awareness of his or her own thinking so that they experience a deeper understanding, not just you. The big idea is NOT to finish the sheet or find the correct answers, (though finishing the sheet with correct answers helps crystalize concepts). Rather, it is to cause the student to change his or her own thinking through mediation (MLE). You must be very intentional in your responses/questioning to increase this awareness and empower the student. Catch them being brilliant or notice when they are doing something desired. For example, "I noticed you didn't erase that one. You made a plan before beginning which showed a restraint of impulsivity."

Remember, the ultimate goal is to empower the student to develop the ability to mediate themselves.

IE Survival Guide
Categorization

<u>Goal</u>
Categorization is about organizing our universe into superordinate categories. It's an extension of both *Organization of Dots* (finding order in chaos) and *Comparisons* (recognizing similarities and differences).

<u>Big Ideas:</u>
- Categorization is based on successful comparison.
- Categorization is essential to organize and store information (this is how we park things in our memory).
- You can apply different principles of classification to the same objects to group and regroup them for different purposes.

There is so much potential for mediation on each page of this instrument. What follows are only suggestions. It is important to allow the students' to do their work and to let your observations drive the mediation. For example, if you plan to talk about precision but the students change strategies, notice the change in strategy and make the students aware of that change in strategy. There will be plenty of opportunities to talk about precision on another page.

Cover Page

In my experience, I have realized that I don't need to endlessly repeat the individual pieces of the cover page. In other words, don't spend so much time on each part that you lose students' interest. The following are constructs and ideas for potential discussions. Don't do them all at once since you will have nine more opportunities (one for each instrument) to cover the salient points.

Logo (a thinker) - simple, memorable, visual (you may have the student put their picture here).
Discuss "What does it mean to think?"
- Brainstorm: recalling, remembering, reflecting, making decisions, having ideas, solving problems, planning to do something, imagining, anticipating, and drawing conclusions.

Talk about problem solving. What is involved?
- Make a chart. Do this collectively with your students. Identify the problem, gather information (through our senses – give examples), consider possible courses of action/solutions, make a plan, carry out the plan, and check for accuracy.

Example: I use a hypothetical problem – I need to ride my bike but I can't. What's the problem? Is it the tire? The chain?

Title – *Categorization*

Symbol - Ask the students what they notice. Invite them to hypothesize what the meaning of the symbol (separating things, using a diagram) is.

Slogan - "Just a Moment . . . LET ME THINK!" This remains the same throughout all the Standard Instruments. It conveys an idea of calmness of the mind. We have time to think and thinking takes time. Some answers take more time to think through than others. It is normal/necessary to think before completing a task.

In *Mind Set* Carol Dweck says that people with fixed mind sets believe smart people already know and therefore don't need time to think. However, a person who has a growth mind set believes learning is a process which takes time and effort. This also helps with restraining impulsivity. Encourage students to think before they act/answer.

Pages 1 and 2

Things to Consider
We can remember more when we use classification to organize the information.

Things are classified according to certain parameters.

Work on the Sheet
Use the document camera to project the top on page one on your screen. Give the students two minutes to look at the picture with the goal of remembering all the objects on it. Turn the document camera off. Hand out page two. Students list the items they remember at the top of the page (number one).

Ask students to explain their strategy for remembering the objects – remembering the central figures and things near it, left to right, top to bottom etc. Unless a student uses categorization, you are talking about short term recall here.

Put the picture back up on the screen. Show the whole page. Talk about the categories used. Discuss them, make meaning of them. Count the number of items in each category. Use the rest of page two in your work. Now remove the picture and challenge the students to name all the objects.

Closure - Discussion for Insight
Discuss the success of recalling all the objects once they were categorized. Where else could we use this? For example, a shopping list, to-do list, or elements required in a school project.

Talk about the table. It is a clear and concise way of representing information. It is easier to commit the table to memory than the picture. How is this helpful?

Page 3

Things to Consider
Define the attributes shared by the group. The characteristics must be clearly defined so that the teacher can decide whether an item belongs to the category or not.

Understand what an exception is.

Work on the Sheet
Systematic work - talk about how students worked to be sure they didn't miss or repeat listed words.

Closure - Discussion for Insight
Exceptions are neither good nor bad. They simply do not share the characteristics needed to be included.

Exceptionality is only relevant to a specific group. Any item can be excluded from a group or included in a group depending on the definition of the group. For example, there are exceptions to the rules in spelling and exceptions to driving the speed limit (ambulance).

Things to Consider
Define the essential attributes of categorization.

Everything belongs to a set. The definition of the set determines if the object belongs or not.

Begin to recognize subsets.

Work on the Sheet
This can be a good opportunity for spontaneous dictionary use.

Students have used categorization in their lives and have an intuitive idea about things that belong and don't belong to a group. Here we are trying to get them to recognize and articulate the rules of categorization.

Closure - Discussion for Insight
Build on the idea of "just right sized words" from *Comparisons*. Members we pick for a group should be as universal as possible rather than specific. For example, #18 *Places of Entertainment* – water parks and movie theaters, rather than Oshkosh Cinema or Kalahari or Wilderness Water Park.

Pages 5 and 6

Things to Consider
Use a diagram to organize classification.

Teach these pages thoroughly. They are the basis for understanding the rest of the instrument.

Precise language - have the students change the word "table" to "chart." (You can mention that this instrument has been translated from Hebrew).

Work on the Sheet
Discuss the principle of classification. Small and large have the superordinate label s*ize*. Everything on the same level of the chart is part of the same superordinate principle.

When we classify according to a certain principle, we ignore all other attributes of the objects.

Closure - Discussion for Insight
A diagram can be read from either direction – top to bottom or bottom to top.

We can check our work by reading the diagram backwards – from the product of the classification.

Pages 7 and 8

Things to Consider
Use a diagram (the "tree diagram" from pages five and six, and a new diagram – a grid) to represent information which was presented verbally or in picture format.

Use multiple attributes in categorization.

Work on the Sheet
We find the information in a grid at the intersection of the vertical columns and horizontal rows. The headings of the rows and columns contain the relevant attributes.

Closure - Discussion for Insight
When classifying by more than one principle, it doesn't matter which principle we classify by first. The result will be the same.

Page 9

Things to Consider
This page is similar to page eight but we are working backwards – the result of classification is shown. We must use induction to find the principles.

Work on the Sheet
Don't tell the students what this page is about. When you give them the page and have them scan it, ask them what they notice. Have the students tell you what they see.

A branch indicates a difference. The point of union before a branch shows the commonality.

Closure - Discussion for Insight
Discuss making a hypothesis and checking it.

Page 10

Things to Consider
This page reviews much of what has already been covered. It also changes the orientation of the "tree chart."

Work on the Sheet
What is the advantage of using a "tree chart" in a horizontal orientation? (It gives more space)

Closure - Discussion for Insight
When we classify we describe. When we describe we don't necessarily classify.

A chart is an efficient way of organizing and presenting information.

Pages 11 and 12

Things to Consider
This page has more complexity - students are classifying according to three principles and with more items.

Work on the Sheet
Systematic work is required to make sure students don't miss any items or duplicate items.

The "tree chart" may be challenging for some students. Remind them that each level represents one principle but the principle does not explicitly appear. For example, "color" is not written, but white, black, and blue will all be in one level.

Closure - Discussion for Insight
Sometimes descriptors are relative. For example, consider *big* and *small*. A small elephant is bigger than a big mouse. When we are not given a referent with which to compare an object we may determine the norm. For example, is an elephant big or small? In the absence of a referent we might say big because elephants are bigger than most other mammals.

Pages 13 and 14

Things to Consider
This exercise uses all the skills we have developed – classifying, working systematically, using a diagram – to accomplish a complex task in classification.

Instead of having the students create the diagram on page 13, I give them a large piece of paper (chart paper works nicely).

Work on the Sheet
Have the student work on the sheet.

Closure - Discussion for Insight
There are many ways to classify animals. The rules (animals needing a pool, etc.) define the principles of classification.

If we lack certain background information, we may need to find that information before we can classify. (All students may not know enough about the animal behaviors in all the examples).

Page 15

Things to Consider
This is an AV page. You may or may not choose to use this page depending on your students' needs.

This page provides repeated opportunities for gathering data from a table and making a diagram to display classification.

Work on the Sheet
You could have students encode - limit lengths to short and long and ages to young and old. See if the students can construct a tree diagram with this information.

Closure - Discussion for Insight
Have students discuss what else in life could be classified according to more than one principle.

Pages 16 - 18

Things to Consider
This task is similar to that in pages 13 and 14. However, pages 13 and 14 supplied rules for classification. Page 17 suggests possible principles as there are no rules given. Students are free to find their own principles of classification.

Consider not using page 18. Instead give the students a large piece of paper instead.

Work on the Sheet
You may want to have the students work collaboratively in teams.

Closure - Discussion for Insight
Have each team present their classification chart (expect differences). The team's intent dictates the principles chosen. There is generally more than one way to classify a group of objects. We might prefer one way over others, but different solutions are not necessarily right or wrong.

Pages 19 and 20

Things to Consider
This is a review and summary of the instrument using emotions classified according to type, value, and intensity.

Notice, principles are supplied for these pages.

Work on the Sheet
This exercise might generate a lively discussion about emotions and connect well with Carol Dweck's *Mind Set*.

Closure - Discussion for Insight
Summarize the instrument:
- Find and label the subject of classification by recognizing similarities among items.
- Find precise labels for categories.
- Include items which contain the common attribute, and exclude items which do not.
- Find your own principles for categorization when none are given.
- Use graphic organizers (tree diagrams, tables, grids) to organize and present information.

You may want to use an example such as cleaning up your messy room. The task is overwhelming until you put things into categories.

IE Survival Guide
Numerical Progressions

Goal
Numerical Progressions looks at rules governing change.

Big Ideas:
Looking at rules governing change requires:
- Perceiving change
- Defining/labeling change
- Observing enough to establish a relationship
- Using hypothetical thinking

Mediate a sense of competency and mastery as students generate new information by using rules he/she has deduced.

There is so much potential for mediation on each page of this instrument. What follows are only suggestions. It is important to allow the students' to do their work and to let your observations drive the mediation. For example, if you plan to talk about precision but the students change strategies, notice the change in strategy and make the students aware of that change in strategy. There will be plenty of opportunities to talk about precision on another page

.

Cover Page

In my experience, I have realized that I don't need to endlessly repeat the individual pieces of the cover page. In other words, don't spend so much time on each part that you lose students' interest. The following are constructs and ideas for potential discussions. Don't do them all at once since you will have eight more opportunities (one for each instrument) to cover the salient points.

Logo (a thinker) - simple, memorable, visual (you may have the student put their picture here).
Discuss "What does it mean to think?"
- Brainstorm: recalling, remembering, reflecting, making decisions, having ideas, solving problems, planning to do something, imagining, anticipating, and drawing conclusions.

Talk about problem solving. What is involved?
- Make a chart. Do this collectively with your students. Identify the problem, gather information (through our senses – give examples), consider possible courses of action/solutions, make a plan, carry out the plan, and check for accuracy.

Example: I use a hypothetical problem – I need to ride my bike but I can't. What's the problem? Is it the tire? The chain?

Title – *Numerical Progressions*

Symbol - Ask the students what they notice. Invite them to hypothesize the meaning of the symbol. (Follow up to understand the word <u>predict</u>.) Write it on the board. Ask, "Who predicts? Why predict?" Discuss.
What about the pattern in the box? Can you predict what comes next? Are predictions always right? Do we live in a world where everything is sure?

Slogan - "Just a Moment . . . LET ME THINK!" This remains the same throughout all the Standard Instruments. It conveys an idea of calmness of the mind: We have time to think and thinking takes

time. Some answers take more time to think through than others. It is normal/necessary to think before completing a task.

In *Mind Set* Carol Dweck says that people with fixed mind sets believe smart people already know and therefore don't need time to think. However, a person who has a growth mind set believes learning is a process which takes time and effort. This also helps with restraining impulsivity. Encourage students to think before they act/ answer.

Page 1

Things to Consider
Pages one and two deal with rhythmic patterns and recurring cycles.
- Recognize a cyclic progression, the stable elements of a cycle and the relationship between the elements.
- Determine the formula (rule governing the relationship).
- Become aware of the ability to predict future events from an analysis of past events.
- Practice the scientific method of investigation: form a hypothesis, test the hypothesis, affirm or reject the hypothesis

Work on the Sheet
These are cyclic progressions. Where else do we see this type of progression? Possible answers - days of week, months of year, seasons, or life cycles.

Closure - Discussion for Insight
Discuss any of the bulleted ideas from "Thing to Consider."

Page 2

Things to Consider
This page contains the same concepts as page one but uses numbers rather than symbols.

A formula is a short, precise explanation of a relationship

Work on the Sheet
Ask the students how they know what comes next. They can use a given formula or figure out the formula themselves.

Closure - Discussion for Insight
Some cycles are unlimited. They repeat the same sequence continuously and endlessly. For example, the days of the week, months of the year, cycles of the moon, or the water cycle.

Some cycles are completed within a limited time or space. For example, life cycles (egg, pupa, caterpillar, butterfly), rhythm in music, design in art, or when we say "ready, set, go."

Page 3

Things to Consider
Divergent thinking is encouraged in the search for possible causes for a relationship.

Work on the Sheet
If you know cause and effect, you can predict.
An effect may have many causes.
Cause to effect is more reliable than effect to cause.

Closure - Discussion for Insight
Scientists sometimes work backward to test a hypothesis. If they can't reject the hypothesis then they must consider it a possibility. We must consider all possibilities. This task works to break the fixed mind-set that is often cultivated in school that there is only one correct answer and once that answer has been found we stop seeking new ideas.

Page 4

Things to Consider
This page introduces relationships which have stable and fixed intervals between two events. Resulting progressions are ascending or descending.

Work on the Sheet
The formula describes the relationship, not the operation. Be sure to talk about both parts of the formula (the plus and the number 2, for example.)

Closure - Discussion for Insight
A relationship between two elements might not be enough to determine the relationship. For example, a progression starting 2, 4 might have a formula +2 or it might have a formula x 2. This is where the scientific method comes in. Form a hypothesis, check it, affirm or reject it.

If the relationship between units is stable, then we can not only predict the future, but also describe the past. Use some of the examples on the page to extend the progressions going both ways.

Page 5

Things to Consider
This page is similar to page four.

Work on the Sheet
There are benchmarks for checking hypotheses. For example, 2a: if the hypothesis +4 is correct, the 23 is correct after you add the 19. Example 2b: after writing 10 and 14, ask yourself, "is 18 next? Yes. My hypothesis is correct."

Closure - Discussion for Insight
If we know the relationship (rule), we can construct a progression from only one number or event.

2a and 2b have the same formula yet the progressions are different. Why? When might progressions overlap or have similar parts? This gets at the idea of being able to extend progressions both ways.

Page 6

Things to Consider
Identify ascending and descending progressions.

Work on the Sheet
Have students note the direction of a progression and the rule that governs the progression.

Closure - Discussion for Insight
The same situation can be viewed from either direction.

Things to Consider
Progressions can contain both ascending and descending elements. The two parts of the formula recur in a cycle - one always follows the other.

Work on the Sheet
For a progression with both ascending and descending elements, the progression will be <u>overall ascending</u> or <u>overall descending</u>. If the positive number is greater than the negative number, the progression ascends. If the positive number is less than the negative number, the progression descends.

Closure - Discussion for Insight
Generate examples of overall ascending or descending progressions: family budget – income and house payment.

Number 3 provides an opportunity to discuss hypothetical reasoning and process of elimination. Notice that the progression is overall ascending. 7 and 9 can be eliminated as a possibility because it is smaller than the starting number. 12 is close to 10. By looking at the length of the progression we know the number will be further from 10 than 12.

Page 8

Things to Consider
Introduce a line graph as a picture of the progression. We are switching modalities here – you can see the whole thing.

Work on the Sheet
Graphs are a coexistence of two variables. In a progression, the variables are quantity and position in the progression.

Anticipate problems with the students' ability to construct a line graph. They have had more experience with bar graphs. Emphasize the variable of position in the progression. Each element of the progression needs to be plotted on a successive vertical line of the graph.

Closure - Discussion for Insight
Ask students, "Why graph it?" Answer: "(So you can see the formula - the (ascent) and fall (descent) of the progression."

Line graphs allow us to see change over time. They allow us to compare quickly and easily without doing the mental arithmetic when we see the progression written in numerical form.

Page 9

Things to Consider
More practice using a line graph to represent a progression.

Work on the Sheet
Have students plot the first progression in pencil. Then plot the second progression on the same graph using a different color. It may be helpful to have students use a colored pencil.

Closure - Discussion for Insight
Discuss #3 on the sheet.

Page 10

Things to Consider
Students are asked to independently construct a graph according to a formula the student makes up.

Planning behavior – students need to consider range and units when making the formula.

Work on the Sheet
Talk about planning behavior before students begin.

Closure - **Discussion for Insight**
Our choices are limited by the constraints imposed by reality. For example, making a formula +50 -2 would be difficult to fit on 16 lines given for the graph.

Where in life are our choices limited by reality? Examples might include vacation locations limited by the available budget or a school project limited by time (due date).

Things to Consider
Introduce the concept of neutral numbers - adding or subtracting 0 or multiplying or dividing by 1 causes no change. However, an event <u>did</u> occur. They indicate that something has happened that resulted in no change.

Work on the Sheet
Have students work on the sheet.

Closure - **Discussion for Insight**
There can be difference causes for the same effect. It is not always possible/important to know the exact cause of an effect.

Generate examples of neutral events. For example, letting paint dry between coats. The drying time didn't change the amount of paint, but it was an important event in the process.

Page 12

Things to Consider
This is an AV page that reviews the concepts about finding relationships in progressions. It reviews the different types of progressions and requires students to use the scientific method of forming and checking hypotheses.

Depending on your students' needs you may or may not choose to use the page.

If you use this page, recognize that extending the progressions on numbers 1d and 1g provides a good opportunity to talk about negative numbers.

Work on the Sheet
Have students work on the sheet.

Closure - Discussion for Insight
Review previously taught concepts. What ideas and concepts need further crystallization? Discuss those ideas and concepts with your students.

Page 13

Things to Consider
This is an AV page that reviews the concepts about neutral numbers and constructing line graphs.

Depending on your students' needs, you may or may not choose to use it.

Work on the Sheet
Have students work on the page.

Closure - Discussion for Insight
Discuss #2b. How do you work to ensure that the third number is 12?

Discuss #2b and 2c. The same event can be part of many different progressions. Different progressions can be generated by the same formula. The formula relates to the relationships between the numbers, not to the numbers themselves.

Page 14

Things to Consider
Students must select relevant information.

Students must work systematically.

Work on the Sheet
Students are discriminating between very similar numbers.

Closure - Discussion for Insight
When is it important to discriminate between things that are very similar? Salt and sugar look similar but taste very different. Being off 1/16 of an inch may not be important if you are working with 1 foot, but a floor that is 32 feet wide would be off 2 inches.

Page 15

Things to Consider
Translating from one modality to another - numbers to graphs.

We can plot relationships rather than absolute numbers.

Work on the Sheet
Notice that there are no numbers on the vertical axis. Discuss what each of the lines on the graph mean. The top line shows no change over time. The solid black line shows an overall descending progression.

Closure - Discussion for Insight
We can see trends and rates of change when we plot a relationship.

Page 16

Things to Consider
Explore static and dynamic elements in a progression. Recognize that static elements may exist in a progression (every other element of a progression is the same number) and may or may not affect the changes in the rest of the progression.

Work on the Sheet
When writing a formula which contains a static element, we show the relationship change above and the static element in the progression line. It is important for students to understand why we don't fill in numbers on the progression line when we show a formula with the relationship shown in a circle above - the numbers are variable but they depend on each other. With a static element, we know that particular number appears so we write the number in the formula.

Closure - Discussion for Insight
Discuss the strategy of writing all the static elements in the progression first and going back and treating the rest of the blanks as a regular progression.

Alternately, students might want to explore the formula moving from one number to the next in order. The progression for #2 has a relationship, then, that looks like: -14, +12 ,-12, +10, -10, +8, -8,+6,-6...

39

Page 17

Things to Consider
Cognitive efficiency – switching thinking from task to task. Emphasize the prediction process to figure out the changing types of formulas.

Work on the Sheet
Every time the student approaches the next example, he or she is applying the whole process (hypothesize, test, affirm or reject).

Closure - Discussion for Insight
Discuss: We are developing the **thinking process**, not the **knowing** process. This is a great tie-in with Carol Dweck's *Mind Set*.

Page 18

Things to Consider
This page introduces a new set of rules governing progressions (each number is the sum of the two preceding numbers).

Work on the Sheet
Students work on the page.

Closure - Discussion for Insight
If one hypothesis fails, try another. Don't keep trying the same hypothesis that failed.

We are seeking rules that describe events. We cannot ignore an event because it does not fit our rule.

Page 19

Things to Consider
On this page students describe in words what is happening in a progression.

Work on the Sheet
Students work on the sheet.

Closure - Discussion for Insight
In some instances, verbal modality is not the most efficient way of describing complex information. But in order to communicate or store information, we must be able to translate other modalities into words.

Page 20

Things to Consider

Exploring relationships <u>between</u> relationships (when the change changes).

Work on the Sheet

Have students work on the sheet.

Closure - Discussion for Insight

Mediation of **challenge** is important when students tackle these complex and novel tasks.

Page 21

Things to Consider
Page 21 is an AV page but it provides needed repetition and extension of thinking. I would **not** recommend skipping this page.

Work on the Sheet
#1a requires induction. #1b requires deduction.

Closure - Discussion for Insight
We must keep looking for a stable and predictable relationship. Relationships between relationships can explain things that are not immediately apparent.

Page 22

Things to Consider
Page 22 is an AV page but it provides needed repetition and extension of thinking. I would not recommend skipping it.

Work on the Sheet
Students create a progression with a formula containing a relationship between a relationship. Then (and this is the tricky part) they give clues to enable a peer to decode their progression. What bits of information are needed? What is redundant information? In other words, how much is just enough – not too much and not too little?

Closure - Discussion for Insight
In order to duplicate a progression and the relationship between its elements, we must be given 3 numbers. Either:
1. Three numbers in the progression
2. One number in the progression, one number in the relationship, and one number in the relationship between the relationship
3. Two numbers in the progression and one number in the relationship
4. One number in the progression and two numbers in the relationship

Page 23

Things to Consider
Page 2 is an AV page that provides repeated practice similar to page 22. Depending on student needs, you may or may not use it.

Work on the Sheet
Have students work on the sheet.

Closure - Discussion for Insight
In order to duplicate a progression and the relationship between its elements, we must be given 3 numbers. Either:
1. Three numbers in the progression
2. One number in the progression, one number in the relationship, and one number in the relationship between the relationship
3. Two numbers in the progression and one number in the relationship
4. One number in the progression and two numbers in the relationship

Page 24

Things to Consider
Decode information from a graph - translation from graphic to numeric or verbal.

Work on the Sheet
Students complete the sheet.
Discuss - Can you find the formula by looking at the graph only and not at the numbers?

Closure - Discussion for Insight
Working precisely and systematically.
It is easier to see movement and compare progressions when they are plotted on a graph.

Page 25

Things to Consider
This page returns to stable relationships (see page four) but the relationship changes to multiplication and division.
Students should be able to work independently by this time.
Mediation should be for transfer rather than for the tasks.

Work on the Sheet
Students work on the sheet.

Closure - Discussion for Insight
Generate ideas for transfer. Where else will you use this?

Page 26

Things to Consider
This page provides repeated practice of concepts learned on page 25 but also requires deductive reasoning to complete the progressions.

Work on the Sheet
Students work on the sheet.

Closure - Discussion for Insight
Generate ideas for transfer. Where else will you use this?

Page 27

Things to Consider
This is similar to page 17 and summarizes the instrument.

Cognitive efficiency – switching thinking from task to task. This page emphasizes the prediction process to figure out the changing types of formulas.

Work on the Sheet
Every time the student approaches the next example, he or she is applying the whole process (hypothesize, test, affirm or reject).

Closure - Discussion for Insight
Summarize the instrument. We learned to look for relationships and relationships between relationships to find a rule governing events. We learned to apply the rules in order to predict future events or to describe past events. We refined our ability to use the scientific method (gather relevant information, form a hypothesis, check the hypothesis, affirm it or reject it).

IE Survival Guide
Family Relations

Goal

Family Relations is about **systems**. Preceding instruments built skills that are required for this instrument. Point this out to the students as they work through the instrument. For example, gathering and organizing information, identifying essential characteristics, and the need for precise labeling were introduced in *Organization of Dots*. The concepts of relationship, directionality, and the projection of relationships through representation were acquired in *Orientation in Space I*. The ability to analyze a complex whole into parts and to assemble parts into a whole while viewing each part as its own whole was developed in *Analytic Perception*. Students determined the rule of relationships and projected that rule on to other phenomena in *Numerical Progressions*. This instrument's presentation of hierarchy and temporal sequences provides the basis for *Temporal Relations*.

Big Ideas:
- Flexibility of thinking - realize you are in many different systems and your status in each is different.
- Recognize hierarchy - gain the ability to take a subservient or a leadership role where appropriate.
- Develop an ability to shift roles as necessary.

This instrument tends to get long. There is a lot of repetition built in to it. If your students understand the concepts as you proceed, you may want to do more than one page in a lesson.

Cover Page

In my experience, I have realized that I don't need to belabor the individual pieces of the cover page. In other words don't spend so much time on each part that you lose students' interest. The following are constructs and ideas for potential discussions. Don't do them all at once since you will have seven more opportunities (one for each instrument) to cover the salient points.

Logo (a thinker) - simple, memorable, visual (you may have the student put their picture here).
Discuss "What does it mean to think?"
- Brainstorm: recalling, remembering, reflecting, making decisions, having ideas, solving problems, planning to do something, imagining, anticipating, and drawing conclusions.

Talk about problem solving. What is involved?
- Make a chart- do this collectively with your students: identify the problem, gather information – (through our senses – give examples), consider possible courses of action/solutions, make a plan, carry out the plan, and check for accuracy.

Example: I use a hypothetical problem – I need to ride my bike but I can't. What's the problem? Is it the tire? The chain?

Title – *Family Relations*
A relationship is a connection, link, or bond between two or more things.
A family is a group of different individuals who are connected through blood or legal relationship.
A family is an example of a system in which certain people have a relationship that is fixed.

Symbol - Ask the students what they notice. Invite them to hypothesize what the meaning of the symbol (symbols in this diagram carry meaning) is.

Name some other systems: school, library, or armed forces are examples.

Slogan - "Just a Moment . . . LET ME THINK!" This remains the same throughout all the Standard Instruments. It conveys an idea of calmness of the mind: We have time to think and thinking takes time. Some answers take more time to think through than others. It is normal/necessary to think before completing a task.

In *Mind Set* Carol Dweck says that people with fixed mind sets believe smart people already know and therefore don't need time to think. However, a person who has a growth mind set believes learning is a process which takes time and effort. This also helps with restraining impulsivity. Encourage students to think before they act/ answer.

Page 1

Things to Consider
Look for relevant information.

Male and female symbols introduced.

Work on the Sheet
Students complete the sheet before discussion.

Supply the words to fill in the blanks. Wife, woman, female requires staying within the same level of comparison.

Closure - Discussion for Insight
Mediate an awareness of the changing nature of an individual as suggested by the birth announcement, marriage invitation, and 70th birthday celebration.

Page 2

Things to Consider
This page introduces the code to show family relationships in a chart format.

Work on the Sheet
Students complete the page.

Closure - Discussion for Insight
People can hold several roles in the same system and also be part of many different systems.

There is a hierarchy in family. On the chart, horizontal lines show people on the same level with equal status while vertical lines show rank or position in the system.

Page 3

Things to Consider
Analyze the change that occurs in a system with the introduction of a new member to the system.

Work on the Sheet
Students complete the page.

Closure - Discussion for Insight
Notice that there is no line between Dena and Dan (siblings). They have an indirect relationship, i.e. the relationship comes through the parents.

Page 4

Things to Consider
Define symmetrical and asymmetrical relationships. A relationship is symmetrical if one of its elements can be substituted for another without a change in meaning. For example, John is Dan's brother. Dan is John's brother. Some relationships are deceptive - a brother/sister relationship is symmetrical but might not appear to be. For example, John is Mary's brother but Mary is John's sister. However, we have a word for brother and sister- *sibling*. If you substitute sibling, the statements work. John is Mary's sibling and Mary is John's sibling.

Work on the Sheet
Students complete the page.

Closure - Discussion for Insight
Look at the genealogical chart and define the rules of symmetry and asymmetry in family relations. A vertical line shows a relationship between levels and is asymmetrical. A horizontal line shows a relationship on the same level and is symmetrical.

Page 5

Things to Consider
Complete a blank genealogical chart based on given information.

Work on the Sheet
Students complete the page.

Closure - Discussion for Insight
We impose order by projecting relationships on objects and events. We do this by comparing, classifying, and organizing the categories into systems.
What are some other systems we have?

In all systems there are differences in status and roles. The status is related to the structure of the system while the role relates to the function of the individual. Conflicts may occur when applying status and role from one system to another. For example, you are the oldest child in your family and have a role as caretaker but in the classroom your role is one of equal footing. You may offend other members of the class if you tell them what to do.

Page 6

Things to Consider
Contrast the nuclear family to an extended family.
Changes occur when two families (or systems) join.
Differentiate between blood and legal relationships in a family.

Work on the Sheet
Students complete the page.

Closure - Discussion for Insight
With the addition of another family, the system changes both quantitatively and qualitatively. Family members acquire new roles. For example, who was once a son and brother is now also a husband.

Page 7

Things to Consider
Develop the need for using logical evidence to support one's answer (answering riddles).

Work on the Sheet
Students complete the page.

Closure - Discussion for Insight
Discuss arguing in the sense of convincing others, not fighting. How do you convince others? In some instances, drawing a chart will be helpful. In some instances, speaking with logic will be helpful. We need to accept other's compelling evidence.

Page 8

Things to Consider
Use a grid to display relationships.

Work on the Sheet
Students complete the page.

Closure - Discussion for Insight
Students prove the relationships. "A is to B as C is to D" (syllogisms). Notice they can work horizontally or vertically.

Page 9

Things to Consider
Elaborate on information gathered from various sources.
Show flexibility of thinking by changing the nature of the task.
Infer relationships based on knowledge of status and role.

Work on the Sheet
Students complete the page.

Closure - Discussion for Insight
Identifying the relationship between two individuals in a family system is easy since it is unambiguous and unequivocal. There may be several correct answers when no constraints are given.

Page 10

Things to Consider
This page provides additional practice of concepts already addressed.

Work on the Sheet
Students complete the page.

Closure - Discussion for Insight
An exception (remember from *Categorization*, page three) is an item that does not share the critical attributes necessary for the category.

The same items may be re-categorized according to different attributes.

Page 11

Things to Consider
The verbal modality requires regulation and control of behavior to invest sufficient time to gather and elaborate on information.

Work on the Sheet
Students complete the page.

Closure - Discussion for Insight
Discuss strategies. How many students made a genealogical chart to help consolidate the information?

Statements can be:
- true but not correct (because it does not answer the question asked)
- incorrect because it is not true or because it is only true under certain circumstances
- both true and correct yet only reflect part of the situation

Page 12

Things to Consider
This page has a higher level of abstraction. Members are notated with letters rather than names. Names helped carry gender. Letters require a stronger use of the circle and rectangle symbols.

Work on the Sheet
This page introduces niece and nephew as reciprocal relationships to aunt and uncle. Cousins are symmetrical relationships.

Closure - Discussion for Insight
Discuss symmetrical/asymmetrical relationships. For example, a teacher can call a student by their first name but a student shouldn't call a teacher by their first name (asymmetrical relationship).

Page 13

Things to Consider
Complete a genealogical chart using previous learning about roles and relationships.

Work on the Sheet
Students complete the page.

Closure - Discussion for Insight
Discuss strategies:
Using direct information (#3 and 5)
Needing to work out of order (#2)
Process of elimination (#1 – one grandmother is already given; there is only one spot left for Arthur)

Pages 14 and 15

Things to Consider
Cousins
Think hypothetically and infer relationships.
Complete a table showing reciprocal relationships.

Work on the Sheet
Students complete the pages.

Closure - Discussion for Insight
Describe the four possible combinations of relationships that can result in the role of cousin.

Page 16

Things to Consider
Reduce egocentricity by putting oneself in another's role: "I am…" riddles.

Work on the Sheet
Students complete the page.

Closure - Discussion for Insight
Top of page - hypothetical thinking (if, then) is not only useful for solving problems in daily life, it is also useful in considering possible outcomes of future acts.

Bottom of the page - A task cannot always be completed in the order the information is given.

Page 17

Things to Consider

This page is a review of previously taught concepts. Students should be expected to be able to complete it independently.

Work on the Sheet

Students complete the page.

Closure - Discussion for Insight

Choose any concept from previous discussions.

Page 18

Things to Consider
This page encourages divergent and inferential thinking.
It asks students to distinguish between what is always true and what is possible. All answers should be justified orally.

Work on the Sheet
Students complete the page.
All answers should be justified orally. In the discussion, only one counter example is needed to show that something is not always true. Many possible alternatives should be discussed.

Closure - Discussion for Insight
Arguments – using precise language, adequate verbal tools, and justifying answers with logical evidence.

Page 19

Things to Consider
This page asks students to complete a crossword puzzle as an exercise to review vocabulary and concepts taught. However, there are too many unknown words not related to the instrument. I would recommend skipping this page entirely or letting students construct their own crossword puzzle on the computer using all the relevant terms they've learned so far.

Work on the Sheet

Closure - Discussion for Insight

Page 20

Things to Consider
Explore the in-law relationship

Work on the Sheet
Students complete the page.

Closure - Discussion for Insight
This page concludes the introduction of the various relationships that exist in families. A blood relationship is permanent but can be ignored. A legal relationship is created by law and can be dissolved. When a legal relationship is dissolved, it has repercussions for other family members. For example, a loved uncle through marriage who is seemingly no longer related.

Page 21

Things to Consider
Review and practice the code used in this instrument (genealogical chart).

The instrument seems to get long and repetitive at this point. I suggest moving through these last pages quickly.

Work on the Sheet
Students complete the page.

Closure - Discussion for Insight

Page 22

Things to Consider
Review and practice the code used in this instrument (genealogical chart).

The instrument seems to get long and repetitive at this point. I suggest moving through these last pages quickly.

Work on the Sheet
Students complete the page.

Closure - Discussion for Insight
Bridge to other systems. How can structure be shown in other systems? Imagine a flow chart. Challenge students to make a chart showing the relationships at your school.

Pages 23 - 25

Things to Consider

These pages allow students to show understanding and mastery of the concepts and relationships presented in the instrument.

Work on the Sheet

Students complete the pages or parts of the pages as you deem appropriate.

Closure - Discussion for Insight

We are capable of:
- seeing data
- seeing relationships
- encoding relationships

IE Survival Guide
Temporal Relations

Goal
Temporal Relations is about classifying time and recognizing the movement of time in order to describe and order one's experiences.

Big Ideas:
Time is not a thing – it is an abstract idea. Time exists only as a relationship between two events or ideas. This relationship is the interval, duration, or transition between the units in a continuum. We are not concerned with what happens during the interval but only with the relationship and that relationship exists only in the abstract.
Time is measured with man-defined units whether they are the rotation of the earth, a sundial, analog clock, or heartbeat.

There is so much potential for mediation on each page of this instrument. What follows are only suggestions. It is important to allow the students' to do their work and to let your observations drive the mediation. For example, if you plan to talk about precision but the students change strategies, notice the change in strategy and make the students aware of that change in strategy. There will be plenty of opportunities to talk about precision on another page.

Cover Page

In my experience, I have realized that I don't need to endlessly repeat the individual pieces of the cover page. In other words, don't spend so much time on each part that you lose students' interest. The following are constructs and ideas for potential discussions. Don't do them all at once since you will have six more opportunities (one for each instrument) to cover the salient points.

Logo (a thinker) - simple, memorable, visual (you may have the student put their picture here).
Discuss "What does it mean to think?"

- Brainstorm: recalling, remembering, reflecting, making decisions, having ideas, solving problems, planning to do something, imagining, anticipating, and drawing conclusions.

Talk about problem solving. What is involved?

- Make a chart. Do this collectively with your students. Identify the problem, gather information (through our senses – give examples), consider possible courses of action/solutions, make a plan, carry out the plan, and check for accuracy.

Example: I use a hypothetical problem – I need to ride my bike but I can't. What's the problem? Is it the tire? The chain?

Title – *Temporal Relations*

Symbol - Ask the students what they notice. (day and night depicted in the windows, two clocks which show twelve o'clock). Invite them to hypothesize what the meaning of the symbol is. Representations of time, the same time can mean two different things. Talk about the difference between absolute time as on a clock and approximate time as with the terms dusk or dawn or day and night.

Slogan - "Just a Moment . . . LET ME THINK!" This remains the same throughout all the Standard Instruments. It conveys an idea of calmness of the mind. We have time to think and thinking takes

time. Some answers take more time to think through than others. It is normal/necessary to think before completing a task.

In *Mind Set* Carol Dweck says that people with fixed mind sets believe smart people already know and therefore don't need time to think. However, a person who has a growth mind set believes learning is a process which takes time and effort. This also helps with restraining impulsivity. Encourage students to think before they act/answer.

Page 1

Things to Consider
This page is not difficult for students to complete. It is the discussion that is important.
Discussion points:
- What is time?
- How do we classify it?
- How do we measure it?

Work on the Sheet
Students complete the page.

Closure - Discussion for Insight
Any unit of measure must be standard (accurate, dependable and constant). Show this by comparing units of time with units of other measure on the page.

Time is irreversible. We cannot "turn back the hands of time." Contrast this idea with other measures (measure distance from either end, weigh something and take some out of it if it weighs too much, temperature rises and falls, etc.). Time moves in only one direction. We can use our memory to recall an earlier time, but we cannot go back to that time.

Page 2

Things to Consider
Order temporal units into a hierarchy (*Family Relations*)

Work on the Sheet
Students complete the page.

Discuss the measures of time. Even though these units are based on natural phenomena (the rotation and revolution of the earth) the divisions or units (24 hours, for example) are arbitrary and generated by humans – in their need to organize their lives.

Closure - Discussion for Insight
Discuss the model representing nested sets. Each larger circle subsumes the circle within it. For example, hours include minutes which include seconds. All hierarchies are not nested. You might challenge students to think of examples which would fit and not fit the graphic organizer. For example, measures of volume (pint, quart, and gallon) would fit, while the school hierarchy (student, teacher, principal) would not.

Have students notice that it is possible to complete the graphic from the outside in or the inside out. The results are the same. This is a review of hierarchies from *Family Relations* where we said you can trace the hierarchy from either direction.

Page 3

Things to Consider
Comparing units of time

Work on the Sheet
Students complete the page.
Students recognize what is required to complete the task – converting between units.

Closure - Discussion for Insight
Discuss some of the examples which seem to be straight forward but have room for argument:
- One month › 4 weeks. This is usually true with the exception of February in 3 out of 4 years.
- Half a year = 6 months. This seems true. 6 months are half of 12 months. However, one could argue that if you count the days, the first half of the year, January through June, contains 181 or 182 days while July through December has 184 days. This is an interesting discussion about the salient or relevant information or the intent of the question. It's a good discussion for those who like to argue everything or find a counterexample for everything.
- 52 weeks = or ‹ one year Again, 52 weeks times 7 days per week equals 364 days yet we say there are 52 weeks in a year. The discussion should center on what degree of precision or accuracy is needed or appropriate.

Page 4

Things to Consider
This is a page of classification.

Work on the Sheet
Students complete the page.

Closure - Discussion for Insight
This is an opportunity to review the attributes of classification and different ways to classify while also talking about time.
The members of the different sets can be compared qualitatively, quantitatively, and according to the frequency of their occurrence.

Page 5

Things to Consider
On this page we start dealing with the sequence of time - past, present, future.
We contrast events in our personal lives with events in the world.

Work on the Sheet
Students complete the page.

Closure - Discussion for Insight
Discussion of past, present, future: when we talk about the present, it is already past. A reference to any specific event is a reference to something that has already past or something that has yet to happen, so it exists only as a memory or it doesn't yet exist. So, can we say nothing really exists? Of course not, but have fun playing with these ideas with the students.

Pages 6 and 8

Things to Consider
You may want to teach these pages together. Each page has 3 examples containing 4 pictures which need to be sequenced.

Work on the Sheet
It is helpful to have the students label the columns: A, B, C, D
Students complete the page.

Closure - Discussion for Insight
Discuss the clues that show the sequence. Close attention to detail is required to complete the task. For example in the first example on page 6, some students will argue whether the man is picking the ladder up or putting it down. If one pays close attention to detail, however, one will notice that there are fewer pieces of fruit on the tree in the last column, so that proves the sequence: 2,1,3,4.

On page 8 the sequence depends on whether the ship is coming or going. We probably don't have enough knowledge of ships to know if we are seeing the prow or stern. Either sequence (2,3,1,4 or 4,1,3,2) can be considered correct.

Page 7

Things to Consider
This is an AV page. This page contains the same type of sequencing tasks from pages 6 and 8 but in a verbal modality. Note: You may need to provide some background knowledge if your students are not familiar with concepts such as sowing, reaping, and plowing,

Work on the Sheet
Students complete the page.

Closure - Discussion for Insight
There is potential for rich discussion on this page:
- 1d: gets at the classic "What came first, the chicken or the egg?" problem.
- 1f: some families call meals by different names (breakfast, dinner, supper). Dinner might be the mid-day meal or the evening meal.
- 1h: sequence depends on personal habits.
- 2a and d: the cyclic nature of some sequences.

Page 9

Things to Consider
This is an AV page. It deals with sequencing dates.

Work on the Sheet
Students complete the page.

Closure - Discussion for Insight
Discussion of attention to detail.
Strategies for efficiency (Where do you look first? What's the hierarchy of importance?). You can talk about the continuum of time and introduce BC dates. This offers a good link to negative numbers with the birth of Christ being the zero point.

Page 10

Things to Consider
This is a complex page (always say "complex" and not "difficult" to the students). The bottom section is a construction task with many different pieces of information.

Work on the Sheet
Define "time span." Give examples (a football season, school year, etc.).
Students complete the page.

Closure - Discussion for Insight
Discuss and compare student strategies for completing the tasks. Talk about the difficulties and how they were overcome.

Page 11

Things to Consider
Order the same elements in different ways.

Work on the Sheet
Students may not know the birthdates of members of their families. You may need to assign getting the birthdates as homework. Students without the necessary information can make up a fictional family.

Students complete the page.

Closure - Discussion for Insight
Discuss the difference between earliest and eldest in ordering. For example, the oldest person may not have joined the family first. Younger people might have married before older people.
In preparing to send birthday or anniversary gifts, age doesn't matter but month of year does.

Page 12

Things to Consider

This is an AV page reviewing ordering events. This page is similar in task and discussion potential to pages 6 – 8. Depending on the needs of your students you may choose to use it or not.

Work on the Sheet

Students complete the page.

Closure - Discussion for Insight

Page 13

Things to Consider
This page is about the perception of time.

Work on the Sheet
You may want to cut the pages apart and give only the half the students will be working on.
Students complete the page (3 minutes for each task).

Closure - Discussion for Insight
Discuss why the same period of time can seem long or short.
In task A we said "try to work as quickly as you can." This might have made the student feel rushed, like there was not enough time. In task B, saying "take your time, do not hurry" might have given the feeling that there was plenty of time. However, people who enjoy math might have a different perception of the time.
Perception of time involves the content of the activity, the level of complexity, level of difficulty, and level of challenge to the individual. The motivation, interest, capacity and attitude of the individual varies from individual to individual and will affect the perception of time.

Page 14

Things to Consider
This page is an extension of the ideas developed with page 13. It gives specific examples of varied motivation, interest, capacity and attitude.

Work on the Sheet
Students complete the page.

Closure - Discussion for Insight
Extend the discussion from page 13. Also recognize that the same span of time can seem both long and short to the individual. The school year might seem to be passing slowly in January and but seem to have passed quickly in June.

Page 15

Things to Consider
How precise do we need to be in talking about time?

Work on the Sheet
Students complete the page.

Closure - Discussion for Insight
What degree of precision is needed in different situations?

Can you tell when precision matters and when it doesn't matter? Only then can you appreciate the importance of precision.

Page 16

Things to Consider
Determine how much information is necessary for the successful completion of a task.

Work on the Sheet
Students complete the page.

Closure - Discussion for Insight
It is fun to let the students create their own example of a birthday party invitation or other event.

Page 17

Things to Consider
This is an AV page reviewing pages 15 and 16. Depending on the needs of your students you may choose to use it or not.

Work on the Sheet
Students complete the page.

Closure - Discussion for Insight
Lead a discussion of ideas from the last two pages that need more attention.

Page 18

Things to Consider
This page explores the idea of relationship between two events: are they coincidences or is there a cause and effect?

Work on the Sheet
Students complete the page.

Closure - Discussion for Insight
Discuss various causes and effects. Encourage divergent thinking. Example 4 seems like cause and effect:
- The bus stopped.
- Many people were waiting at the station.

While recognizing there is a strong possibility for cause and effect, there are other possibilities (the car in front of the bus stopped, or a squirrel ran in front of the bus).

Page 19

Things to Consider
Look at the differences between time, distance, and speed.
This page is used to develop the language.

Work on the Sheet
Students complete the page.

Closure - Discussion for Insight
Speed is the intersection of time and space – a relationship between two relationships (time being the relationship between two events and space being the relationship between two places).

Page 20

Things to Consider
Time, speed, and distance are interrelated and dependent on each other. For example, increasing distance will increase time if speed is constant. (This is the first of 4 pages that deal with these ideas)

Work on the Sheet
Students complete the page.

Closure - Discussion for Insight
We are applying logic to symbolic relationships.
Give examples of the relationships between distance, speed, and time (increasing distance will increase time if the speed is constant).

Page 21

Things to Consider
Extending the ideas developed with page 20.

Work on the Sheet
Students complete the page.

Closure - Discussion for Insight
Having the same beginning and ending point does not guarantee the same distance or the same travel time.

Pages 22 and 23

Things to Consider
Use symbolic data to show universal relationships.

Work on the Sheet
On page 22 have the students encode the information:
1. first day is A, second day is B
2. X is A and Y is B
3. Small car is A and big car is B
4. X is A and Y is B
5. Ellen is A and Bess is B
6. Turtle A and Turtle B are already labeled

This helps with page 23 and filling in the chart with A and B.

Closure - Discussion for Insight
Summarize the whole instrument. Have the students create a mind map of concepts learned.

IE Survival Guide
Illustrations

<u>Goal</u>
Illustrations is used during our circle time in the morning to pose situations that have real life application.

<u>Big Ideas:</u>
- Novel solutions to problem solving
- Recognizing absurdity
- Point of view – reflective thinking

There is so much potential for mediation on each page of this instrument. What follows are only suggestions. It is important to allow the students' to do their work and let your observations drive the mediation. For example, if you plan to talk about precision but the students change strategies, notice the change in strategy and make the students aware of that change in strategy. There will be plenty of opportunities to talk about precision on another page.

Cover Page

In my experience, I have realized that I don't need to belabor the individual pieces of the cover page. In other words don't spend so much time on each part that you lose students' interest. The following are constructs and ideas for potential discussions. Don't do them all at once since you will have five more opportunities (one for each instrument) to cover the salient points.

Logo (a thinker) - simple, memorable, visual (you may have the student put their picture here).
Discuss "What does it mean to think?"
- Brainstorm: recalling, remembering, reflecting, making decisions, having ideas, solving problems, planning to do something, imagining, anticipating, and drawing conclusions.

Talk about problem solving. What is involved?
- Make a chart- do this collectively with your students: identify the problem, gather information – (through our senses – give examples), consider possible courses of action/solutions, make a plan, carry out the plan, and check for accuracy.

Example: I use a hypothetical problem – I need to ride my bike but I can't. What's the problem? Is it the tire? The chain?

Title – *Illustrations*

Symbol - Ask the students what they notice (man with a red face and a man painting a fence). Invite them to hypothesize the meaning of the symbol. Talk about the disequilibrium between the two people (someone who is mad and one who is contentedly painting). Have them identify or infer the problem and the relationship between the people. Then devise a solution.

Slogan - "Just a Moment . . . LET ME THINK!" This remains the same throughout all the Standard Instruments. It conveys an idea of calmness of the mind: We have time to think and thinking takes

time. Some answers take more time to think through than others. It is normal/necessary to think before completing a task.

In *Mind Set* Carol Dweck says that people with fixed mind sets believe smart people already know and therefore don't need time to think. However, a person who has a growth mind set believes learning is a process which takes time and effort. This also helps with restraining impulsivity. Encourage students to think before they act/ answer.

Pages 1- 2

Things to Consider
These pages are not difficult for students to complete. There is a moral to the story and requires reflective thinking.

Work on the Sheet
Page 1 – Have students note the input (bubble) so they are able to infer what is going on.

Page 2 – Talk about the elements of a plan.

Closure - Discussion for Insight
Page 1 – Ask the students, "Which frog are they and why." A possible moral of the story is, "If you don't believe you can do something, you never will."

Page 2 – When would you try and get two opposing forces together?

Page 3

Things to Consider
Sometimes solutions require looking at things in a different way.

Work on the Sheet
Make sure the students have the page in the correct orientation.

Closure - Discussion for Insight
    When is it a good idea to solve a problem that might be daring?
    Have you ever solved a problem only to create another one?

Page 4

Things to Consider
This page is about the relationship between reality and perception.

Work on the Sheet
Students complete the page.

Closure - Discussion for Insight
Discuss some of the examples of how we draw conclusions as a result of our perceptions.

Page 5

Things to Consider
This is a page about point of view.

Work on the Sheet
Have students look at the page (in sequence)

Closure - Discussion for Insight
Have the students tell the story from different viewpoints.
You may also ask the students, "Which dog are you?" Have them tell you why.

Page 6

Things to Consider
This page is about a novel solution to a problem.

Work on the Sheet
Students complete the page.

Closure - Discussion for Insight
Ask the students if they think the cat made a hypothesis before he made the decision to run across the board.

When do decisions require a quick review of solutions before proceeding?

Page 7

Things to Consider
Have an understanding of explicit and implicit information.

Work on the Sheet
Have students describe the sheet and point out which cues are implicit and explicit.

Closure - Discussion for Insight
Ask students how we evaluate our own decisions and how we attain our goals. Who/what influences those decisions?

Page 8

Things to Consider
This is another page about perception of reality.

Work on the Sheet
Students look at the page.

Closure - Discussion for Insight
When is it valuable to compare ourselves to others? Do we see ourselves more realistically?

Pages 9 - 10

Things to Consider
These are pages that have a creative solution to a problem.

Work on the Sheet
Students look at the page.

Closure - Discussion for Insight
Do we anticipate the consequences to a unique or creative solution?
When would you consider something to be high risk?

Page 11

Things to Consider
This is an absurd page where students have to define the problem and determine the source of the problem.

Work on the Sheet
Have students analyze both of the pictures and compare the solutions.

Closure - Discussion for Insight
How did you describe the problem? Did the description give you cues/clues to the solution? Has someone else's problem ever been passed on to become your problem?

Page 12

Things to Consider
Make sure to check the orientation. This is a picture where the solution is absurd.

Work on the Sheet
Have students describe the page.

Closure - Discussion for Insight
Have you ever made a decision where you can't have a do over?

Page 13

Things to Consider
Make sure to check the orientation. This page does not really solve the problem.

Work on the Sheet
Students look at the page.

Closure - Discussion for Insight
Did the solution solve the problem? Even though it looks like the problem was solved, is the solution going to help him in the future? Is he just fooling himself?

Page 14

Things to Consider
This page is about perception vs reality.

Work on the Sheet
Have the students sequentially follow the story and describe what they see in each frame.

Closure - Discussion for Insight
Ask the students if what they are anticipating is really reality (positive and negative). How much does your attitude determine how you see things?

Page 15

Things to Consider
This page is about an absurd sequence of events. Notice the large case and the small violin.

Work on the Sheet
Students compare the frames on the page.

Closure - Discussion for Insight
When have we looked at an outward appearance such as the large case and made false conclusions?

Page 16

Things to Consider
This page is another absurdity. Notice the man shooting the gun upward and the dog bringing him a fish.

Work on the Sheet
Students describe the page.

Closure - Discussion for Insight
When have you gotten something unexpected from your efforts?

Page 17

Things to Consider
This page is about the need to define a problem.

Work on the Sheet
Students describe the page.

Closure - Discussion for Insight
If two things are similar, how easy is it to make errors? When have you taken more amount of time before making a big decision?

Page 18

Things to Consider
This is an absurd page where one needs to consider how their decision affects others.

Work on the Sheet
Students look at the page and compare the result of their action.

Closure - Discussion for Insight
Lead a discussion about being overloaded. Ask what causes a breaking point.

Page 19

Things to Consider
This page is about an absurdity and one's actions can cause an even worse problem.

Work on the Sheet
Students look at the page and compare the frames.

Closure - Discussion for Insight
Talk about something that may be funny to others, e.g. unexpectedly falling out of one's chair but not funny to the person it happens to. What decision(s) can worsen or improve the situation?

Page 20

Things to Consider
This is yet another sheet about planning and thinking before you act.

Work on the Sheet
Have students look at the story.

Closure - Discussion for Insight
Can you name a time when your planning turned something into a worse situation?

www.ingramcontent.com/pod-product-compliance
Lightning Source LLC
Chambersburg PA
CBHW020950230426
43666CB00005B/255